" The Best Game Changer Sales Solution"

INTRODUCTIO...

Introducing the "The Best Game Changer Sales Solution" e-book, the ultimate guide to revolutionizing your sales strategy and achieving unparalleled success. This comprehensive e-book offers valuable insights, tips, and strategies to help you streamline your sales process, increase your revenue, and outperform your competitors.

In today's fast-paced business environment, sales teams face constant challenges to meet their targets and exceed expectations. The "The Best Game Changer Sales Solution" e-book is designed to help sales professionals at every level to overcome these challenges and achieve their goals. Whether you are a seasoned sales veteran or just starting out, this e-book provides practical and actionable advice that will transform your sales approach.

The "The Best Game Changer Sales Solution" e-book covers a wide range of topics, including lead generation, effective communication, building strong relationships with customers, and closing deals. It also includes cutting-edge techniques for leveraging the latest technologies and tools to optimize your sales process and maximize your results.

With its engaging writing style and clear, concise advice, the "The Best Game Changer Sales Solution" e-book is the ultimate resource for sales professionals who want to take their performance to the next level. Whether you work in a small business or a large corporation, this e-book will provide you with the tools and strategies you need to succeed in today's highly competitive sales landscape. So why wait? Get your copy of the "The Best Game Changer Sales Solution" e-book today and start transforming your sales approach!

INDEX

Here are 15 different chapter covered in the "Game Changer Sales Solution" e-book:

1.Lead generation strategies :

2.Effective communication techniques :

3.Building strong relationships with customers :

4.Closing deals and overcoming objections:

5.Social proof and testimonials :

6.Personalization and customization in sales:

7.Creating a sense of urgency in sales :

8.Leveraging technology for sales success :

9.Tracking and analyzing sales performance data :

10.Developing a strong brand image and reputation :

11.Staying up-to-date with the latest sales trends and techniques:

12.The importance of active listening in sales :

13.Using data and analytics to make informed sales decisions :

14.Staying motivated and focused in sales :

15.Overcoming common sales challenges and obstacles :

Each of these Chapter is explored in-depth in the " The Best Game Changer Sales Solution" e-book, providing practical tips, strategies, and insights that sales professionals at every level can use to improve their performance and achieve their goals. Whether you are new to sales or have years of experience, this e-book offers valuable guidance and advice to help you stand out from the competition and succeed in today's highly competitive sales landscape.

CHAPTER :- 1

Lead generation strategies :

Lead generation is the process of identifying and attracting potential customers for your business. It is an essential part of any successful marketing strategy. Without leads, a business cannot grow and thrive. In this chapter, we will discuss some of the most effective lead generation strategies that businesses can use to attract potential customers.

1.Content Marketing.
Content marketing involves creating valuable and informative content that can attract potential customers to your business. It is a great way to establish your authority and expertise in your industry. By creating useful content, you can attract potential customers who are searching for information about

your products or services. This can help you generate leads that are more likely to convert into paying customers.

2.Social Media Marketing.
Social media marketing involves using social media platforms such as Facebook, Twitter, and LinkedIn to connect with potential customers. By creating engaging content and sharing it on social media, businesses can attract potential customers and generate leads. Social media also allows businesses to engage with their customers and build relationships that can lead to more sales.

3.Search Engine Optimization (SEO)
Search engine optimization (SEO) is the process of optimizing your website and content for search engines. By improving your website's visibility in search results, you can attract more potential customers to your website. SEO involves optimizing your website's content, meta descriptions, and keywords to improve its ranking in search results.

4.Pay-Per-Click (PPC) Advertising .
Pay-per-click (PPC) advertising involves placing ads on search engines or social media platforms and paying each time someone clicks on your ad. PPC advertising is a great way to attract potential customers who are searching for your products or services. By targeting specific keywords and demographics, businesses can generate leads that are more likely to convert into paying customers.

5.Email Marketing.
Email marketing involves sending promotional emails to potential customers who have opted-in to receive them. By providing useful and engaging content, businesses can build relationships with potential customers and encourage them to

take action. Email marketing can be a great way to generate leads and convert them into paying customers.

6.Referral Marketing.

Referral marketing involves encouraging your existing customers to refer their friends and family to your business. By offering incentives such as discounts or free products, businesses can encourage their customers to refer others. Referral marketing is a great way to generate leads that are more likely to convert into paying customers because they have been recommended by someone they trust.

7.Events and Trade Shows.

Events and trade shows are great opportunities for businesses to showcase their products or services and generate leads. By attending industry events and trade shows, businesses can connect with potential customers and build relationships. Events and trade shows also allow businesses to gather valuable feedback and insights that can help them improve their products or services.

In conclusion, there are many effective lead generation strategies that businesses can use to attract potential customers. By using a combination of these strategies, businesses can generate leads that are more likely to convert into paying customers. It's important to remember that lead generation is an ongoing process, and businesses should constantly evaluate and improve their strategies to ensure continued success.

CHAPTER :- 2

Effective communication techniques :

Effective communication is essential for success in any field, and sales is no exception. In fact, effective communication skills are crucial for sales professionals to connect with customers, understand their needs and motivations, and build lasting relationships. In this chapter, we will explore some of the most important effective communication techniques that can help sales professionals improve their performance and achieve their goals.

1.Active Listening:
The Art of Listening to Understand
Active listening is a fundamental communication technique that involves giving your full attention to the person speaking and demonstrating that you understand what they are saying. To be an effective listener, you must focus on the speaker, ask clarifying questions, and avoid interrupting or making assumptions. Active listening helps build rapport and trust with customers, as it shows that you value their input and are committed to understanding their needs.

2.Empathetic Communication: Understanding and Connecting with the Customer's Emotions

Empathetic communication involves understanding and connecting with the customer's emotions. To be empathetic, you must be aware of the customer's feelings, acknowledge their emotions, and respond appropriately. This technique can be particularly effective when dealing with customers who are anxious or frustrated, as it can help de-escalate tense situations and build rapport.

3.Asking Open-Ended Questions:

Encouraging the Customer to Share More Information Asking open-ended questions is an effective technique for encouraging the customer to share more information. Open-ended questions cannot be answered with a simple "yes" or "no" and instead require the customer to provide more detail. This technique can help you understand the customer's needs, preferences, and motivations more fully, which can in turn help you provide more effective solutions.

4.Mirroring:

Reflecting the Customer's Language, Tone, and Body Language Mirroring involves reflecting the customer's language, tone, and body language to build rapport and establish trust. This technique can help put the customer at ease and create a sense of familiarity, which can in turn make them more receptive to your message.

5.Tactful Interruption: Gently Interrupting the Customer to Redirect the Conversation
Tactful interruption involves gently interrupting the customer to redirect the conversation. This technique can be effective when the conversation has gone off track or when the customer is discussing irrelevant or unrelated topics. To be tactful, you must interrupt in a polite and respectful manner and be clear about the purpose of the interruption.

6.Paraphrasing: Restating the Customer's Words in Your Own Words
Paraphrasing involves restating the customer's words in your own words to ensure that you have understood their message correctly. This technique can help you avoid misunderstandings and build rapport with the customer.

7.Summarizing:
Briefly Summarizing the Conversation to Ensure Understanding
Summarizing involves briefly summarizing the conversation to ensure that you have understood the customer's needs and preferences correctly. This technique can help you avoid misunderstandings and ensure that you are on the same page as the customer.

8.Clear and Concise Language:
Using Simple, Jargon-Free Language to Avoid Confusion
Clear and concise language involves using simple, jargon-free language to avoid confusion. This technique can be particularly effective when dealing with customers

who are not familiar with technical or industry-specific terms. By using clear and concise language, you can ensure that the customer understands your message and can make an informed decision.

9.Positive Language: Using Optimistic and Solution-Focused Language

Positive language involves using optimistic and solution-focused language to build rapport and encourage the customer to take action. This technique can be particularly effective when dealing with customers who are hesitant or unsure about making a purchase.

10.Nonverbal Communication:

Paying Attention to Body Language, Tone of Voice, and Facial Expressions

Nonverbal communication involves paying attention to body language, tone of voice, and facial expressions to understand the customer's emotions and respond appropriately. This technique can be particularly useful when dealing with customers who may not be vocal about their feelings. By paying attention to nonverbal cues, you can adjust your approach and tailor your message to the customer's needs.

11.Confidence:

Projecting Confidence and Authority in Your Communication

Confidence involves projecting confidence and authority in your communication to inspire trust and credibility. This technique can be particularly effective when dealing with customers who may be skeptical or uncertain. By projecting confidence, you can demonstrate that you are knowledgeable and trustworthy, which can make the customer more receptive to your message.

12.Adaptability:
Adapting Your Communication Style to Suit Different Customers
Adaptability involves adapting your communication style to suit different customers. This technique can be particularly useful when dealing with customers from different cultures or with different communication preferences. By adapting your communication style, you can build rapport and establish trust with a wider range of customers.

13.Clarity:
Being Clear and Concise in Your Communication
Clarity involves being clear and concise in your communication to avoid confusion and ensure that the customer understands your message. This technique can be particularly useful when discussing complex products or services. By being clear and concise, you can help the customer make an informed decision.

14.Respectful Language: Using Respectful Language to Build Rapport and Trust
Respectful language involves using respectful language to build rapport and trust with the customer. This technique can be particularly effective when dealing with customers who may have different values or beliefs. By

using respectful language, you can demonstrate that you value the customer's perspective and are committed to building a positive relationship.

15.Follow-Up:
Following Up with Customers to Ensure Satisfaction and Address Any Concerns
Follow-up involves following up with customers after the sale to ensure satisfaction and address any concerns they may have. This technique can be particularly effective for building long-term relationships with customers. By following up,you can demonstrate that you care about the customer's experience and are committed to providing excellent service.

In conclusion, effective communication is critical for sales professionals who want to build lasting relationships with customers and achieve their goals. By using these effective communication techniques, sales professionals can improve their performance, build rapport and trust with customers, and ultimately, drive sales success.

CHAPTER :- 3

Building strong relationships with customers :

Building strong relationships with customers is critical for businesses that want to succeed in today's competitive marketplace. Strong customer relationships can lead to repeat business, positive word-of-mouth advertising, and increased revenue. In this chapter, we will discuss several tips step by steps for building strong relationships with customers.

1.Be Responsive: Respond to Customer Inquiries and Concerns Quickly.

Being responsive is essential for building strong relationships with customers. Customers expect timely responses to their inquiries and concerns, and failure to respond quickly can damage the relationship. Sales professionals should make every effort to respond to customer inquiries and concerns promptly, even if they do not have an immediate solution.

2.Personalize Communication:
Address Customers by Name and Personalize Your Messages.

Personalizing communication can help build strong relationships with customers. Sales professionals should address customers by name and tailor their messages to suit the customer's needs and preferences. By personalizing communication, sales professionals can demonstrate that they value the customer's individuality and are committed to providing excellent service.

3.Listen to Feedback: Solicit and Act on Customer Feedback.

Listening to feedback is critical for building strong relationships with customers. Sales professionals should solicit customer feedback regularly and use it to improve their products and services. By acting on customer feedback, sales professionals can demonstrate that they value the customer's opinions and are committed to providing high-quality products and services.

4.Follow Through:
Deliver on Promises and Follow Through on Commitments.

Following through on promises is essential for building strong relationships with customers. Sales professionals should deliver on their promises and follow through on their commitments. By following through, sales professionals can demonstrate that they are reliable and trustworthy, which can help build long-term customer relationships.

5.Build Rapport:
Establish a Personal Connection with Customers.

Building rapport is essential for building strong relationships with customers. Sales professionals should try to establish a personal connection with customers by asking about their interests and showing an interest in their lives outside of the sales transaction. By building rapport, sales professionals can create a more relaxed and trusting relationship with customers.

6.Provide Value:
Offer Value-Added Services and Information.

Providing value is critical for building strong relationships with customers. Sales professionals should offer value-added services and information that can help customers achieve their goals. By providing value, sales professionals can demonstrate their expertise and commitment to customer success.

7.Be Honest:
Be Transparent and Honest in Your Communication.

Being honest is essential for building strong relationships with customers. Sales professionals should be transparent and honest in their communication, even if it means admitting mistakes or acknowledging shortcomings. By being honest, sales professionals can build trust and credibility with customers.

8.Anticipate Needs: Anticipate and Respond to Customer Needs.

Anticipating customer needs is essential for building strong relationships with customers. Sales professionals should try to anticipate customer needs and respond proactively. By anticipating needs, sales professionals can demonstrate their commitment to customer satisfaction.

9.Provide Excellent Service:

Provide Consistently High-Quality Service.

Providing excellent service is critical for building strong relationships with customers. Sales professionals should strive to provide consistently high-quality service that meets or exceeds customer expectations. By providing excellent service, sales professionals can build loyalty and repeat business.

10.Be Empathetic:
Show Empathy and Understanding in Your Interactions with Customers.

Being empathetic is essential for building strong relationships with customers. Sales professionals should show empathy and understanding in their interactions with customers, especially when dealing with difficult or sensitive issues. By being empathetic, sales professionals can create a more positive and supportive relationship with customers.

In conclusion, building strong relationships with customers is critical for business success. By following these tips, sales professionals can improve their relationship-building skills, build rapport and trust with customers, and ultimately, drive business growth.

CHAPTER :- 4

Closing deals and overcoming objections:

Closing deals and overcoming objections are two critical aspects of the sales process. While closing a deal is about getting the customer to make a purchase, overcoming objections is about addressing any concerns or doubts that the customer may have about the product or service. In this chapter, we will outline the steps involved in both closing deals and overcoming objections.

Closing Deals:

1.Build Rapport:
Building rapport with the customer is an essential first step in the sales process. Establishing a connection with the customer can help you build trust and credibility, which can ultimately lead to a successful sale.

2.Identify Needs:
Once you have built rapport with the customer, it's time to identify their needs. Ask open-ended questions to understand their pain points, goals, and aspirations. This will help you tailor your pitch to their specific needs.

3.Present Solutions: After identifying the customer's needs, present solutions that align with their goals and address their pain points. Explain the benefits of your product or service and how it can solve their problems.

4.Overcome Objections: It's common for customers to have objections during the sales process. Address these objections by providing evidence or testimonials from satisfied customers. If the objection is related to price, you can offer a discount or payment plan.

5.Close the Deal:
Once you have addressed all the customer's objections and presented the benefits of your product or service, it's time to close the deal. Ask for the sale by using a closing statement such as "Would you like to place an order now?" or "When would you like to get started?"

Overcoming Objections:

1.Listen:
When a customer raises an objection, it's important to listen carefully to what they're saying. Don't interrupt or argue with the customer. Instead, try to understand their concerns and show empathy.

2.Clarify:
Once you have listened to the customer's objection, clarify their concern. Restate their objection in your own words to ensure that you have understood their concern correctly.

3.Address the Concern: After clarifying the concern, address it directly. Provide evidence or testimonials from satisfied customers that demonstrate the benefits of your product or service. If the concern is related to price, offer a discount or payment plan.

4.Ask for Feedback:
After addressing the customer's concern, ask for feedback to ensure that they are satisfied with your response. If the customer is still not convinced, ask for specific feedback on what you can do to address their concern.

5.Follow Up:
It's important to follow up with the customer after addressing their concern. This shows that you care about their satisfaction and are committed to ensuring that they are happy with their purchase.

In conclusion, closing deals and overcoming objections are two critical aspects of the sales process. By building rapport, identifying needs, presenting solutions, and addressing objections, you can successfully close a deal. When addressing objections, it's important to listen, clarify, address the concern, ask for feedback, and follow up. With these steps, you can overcome objections and increase your chances of closing a successful sale.

Additional Tips :
Here are some additional details and tips for closing deals and overcoming objections:

Closing Deals:

1.Build Rapport:

Building rapport with the customer is key to establishing trust and credibility. This can be achieved by showing genuine interest in the customer and their needs. Use active listening skills, such as asking follow-up questions and repeating back what the customer has said, to demonstrate that you are actively engaged in the conversation.

2.Identify Needs:

To effectively identify the customer's needs, ask open-ended questions that allow them to explain their situation and what they're looking for. Use this information to tailor your pitch and present solutions that meet their specific needs.

3.Present Solutions: When presenting solutions, focus on the benefits of your product or service. Use concrete examples to demonstrate how your product or service can solve the customer's problems or help them achieve their goals. Avoid using jargon or technical language that the customer may not understand.

4.Overcome Objections: When addressing objections, it's important to remain calm and professional. Don't take the objection personally or become defensive. Instead, acknowledge the customer's concern and provide evidence or examples to address their objection.

5.Close the Deal:

To close the deal, use a closing statement that is clear and direct. Avoid using pushy or aggressive tactics, as this can make the customer feel uncomfortable or pressured. Instead, use a closing statement that is friendly and respectful, such as "I think our product would be a great fit for your needs. Can we move forward with an order?"

Overcoming Objections:

1.Listen:
When a customer raises an objection, it's important to listen carefully to what they're saying. Don't interrupt or dismiss their concerns. Instead, show empathy and try to understand their perspective.

2.Clarify:
After the customer has raised an objection, clarify their concern to ensure that you have understood it correctly. Restate their objection in your own words, and ask the customer if your understanding is accurate.

3.Address the Concern: When addressing the customer's concern, be specific and provide evidence or examples to support your response. Avoid making generalizations or promises that you can't keep. If the concern is related to price, consider offering a discount or payment plan.

4.Ask for Feedback: After addressing the customer's concern, ask for feedback to ensure that they are satisfied with your response. This can help you identify any additional concerns that the customer may have and address them proactively.

5.Follow Up:
Following up with the customer after addressing their concern is a critical step in building a long-term relationship. This can help you establish trust and credibility with the customer, and increase the likelihood of future sales.

Overall, closing deals and overcoming objections require patience, persistence, and a customer-centric approach. By focusing on the customer's needs, listening actively, and addressing concerns proactively, you can increase your chances of closing successful sales and building long-term relationships with your customers.

CHAPTER :- 5

Social proof and testimonials :

Social proof and testimonials are powerful marketing tools that businesses use to persuade potential customers to buy their products or services. They provide evidence that other people have used and benefited from a product or service, making it more attractive to others. In this chapter, we'll provide a step-by-step guide to using social proof and testimonials in your marketing strategy.

Step 1: Understand Social Proof :

Social proof is a psychological phenomenon in which people rely on the actions and opinions of others to guide their own behavior. It is a form of social influence, and it is used extensively in marketing to persuade people to buy products or services. Social proof can take many forms, such as customer reviews, celebrity endorsements, and social media likes and shares.

Step 2: Identify Your Target Audience :

Before you can use social proof and testimonials effectively, you need to know who your target audience is. Who are your ideal customers? What do they care about? What are their pain points? Once you have a clear understanding of your target audience, you can tailor your social proof and testimonials to appeal to them.

Step 3: Gather Testimonials :

Testimonials are an essential part of social proof. They provide real-world examples of how your product or service has helped others. To gather testimonials, reach out to your existing customers and ask them to share their experiences. You can also offer incentives for customers to provide testimonials, such as discounts or free products.

When gathering testimonials, be sure to ask specific questions that will elicit detailed responses. For example, ask customers to describe the problem they were facing before they used your product or service, how your product or service helped them solve the problem, and what specific results they achieved.

Step 4: Choose the Right Platform :

Once you have gathered testimonials, you need to decide where to display them. There are many platforms you can use, including your website, social media, and third-party review sites. Choose the platforms that are most relevant to your target audience.

Step 5: Display Testimonials Effectively:

How you display your testimonials is just as important as the testimonials themselves. Here are a few tips to help you display your testimonials effectively:

*Use visuals:
Visuals, such as photos or videos of customers using your product or service, can make your testimonials more engaging and memorable.

*Highlight key quotes: Pull out the most compelling quotes from your testimonials and display them prominently on your website or social media.

*Use social proof widgets:
Social proof widgets are third-party tools that display customer reviews and ratings on your website. They can be an effective way to showcase social proof.

Step 6: Leverage Social Media :

Social media is a powerful platform for social proof. You can use social media to showcase customer reviews, highlight customer success stories, and share user-generated content. Be sure to monitor your social media accounts for mentions and reviews, and respond promptly to any negative feedback.

Step 7: Continuously Gather and Update Testimonials :

Social proof is not a one-time effort. You need to continuously gather and update testimonials to keep your marketing strategy fresh and relevant. Encourage customers to provide feedback on an ongoing basis, and regularly refresh your social proof content.

In conclusion, social proof and testimonials are powerful marketing tools that can help you persuade potential customers to buy your products or services. By understanding social proof, identifying your target audience, gathering testimonials, choosing the right platform, displaying testimonials effectively, leveraging social media, and continuously gathering and updating testimonials, you can create a successful social proof strategy that drives sales and builds trust with your audience.

Additional Tips :

Here are some additional tips and strategies for using social proof and testimonials effectively:

*Use a Variety of Testimonial Types.
There are many types of testimonials you can use, including written testimonials, video testimonials, case studies, and success stories. By using a variety of testimonial types, you can appeal to different types of customers and provide more diverse evidence of your product or service's value.

*Focus on Specific Benefits.
When gathering and displaying testimonials, focus on specific benefits that your product or service provides. For example, if you sell a weight loss program, focus on testimonials that highlight the program's ability to help people lose weight and feel healthier, rather than general statements about how great the program is.

*Use Social Proof in Your Advertising.
Social proof can be a powerful addition to your advertising campaigns. For example, you can use customer reviews and ratings in your Google Ads, or display social proof widgets on your website's landing pages. By using social proof in your

advertising, you can increase the likelihood that people will click on your ads and convert into paying customers.

***Encourage User-Generated Content.**
User-generated content (UGC) is content created by your customers, such as reviews, photos, and videos. By encouraging UGC and sharing it on your social media accounts and website, you can demonstrate social proof in a more authentic way. UGC is also a great way to build engagement and loyalty with your customers.

***Use Influencers.**
Influencers are individuals with a large following on social media who can help promote your product or service to their followers. Influencer marketing can be a powerful way to leverage social proof, as people trust the opinions of influencers they follow. When working with influencers, be sure to choose individuals who align with your brand values and target audience.

***Be Transparent .**
When using social proof and testimonials, it's important to be transparent and honest about the experiences of your customers. Don't edit or manipulate testimonials to make them sound better than they really are. If you receive negative feedback, respond in a respectful and helpful way. Being transparent and authentic can actually strengthen your social proof, as it demonstrates your commitment to customer satisfaction.

In summary, social proof and testimonials are powerful tools for building trust and driving sales. By using a variety of testimonial types, focusing on specific benefits, using social proof in your advertising, encouraging user-generated content, leveraging influencers, and being transparent, you can create a strong social proof strategy that helps you stand out in a crowded market.

CHAPTER :- 6

Personalization and customization in sales:

Personalization and customization in sales are essential strategies for creating a personalized and tailored experience for each customer. By understanding each customer's unique needs and preferences, you can create a more meaningful and engaging sales process that increases the likelihood of a successful sale. In this chapter, we'll explore some key strategies for personalization and customization in sales.

1.Gather Information About Your Customers.

The first step in personalization and customization is to gather information about your customers. This includes demographic information, such as age, gender, and location, as well as their preferences, interests, and behaviors. You can gather this information through surveys, questionnaires, and customer feedback. Use this information to create customer profiles that can help you understand each customer's needs and preferences.

2.Use Personalized Communication.

Once you have gathered information about your customers, you can use personalized communication to engage with them. This can include addressing them by name in emails, tailoring your messaging to their specific needs and interests, and using their preferred communication channels, such as email, phone, or social media. Personalized communication helps create a more personal and meaningful connection with each customer.

3.Offer Customized Products and Services.

Offering customized products and services is another way to create a personalized experience for your customers. This can include customizing products based on customer preferences, such as color or size, or offering personalized services based on customer needs. For example, if you offer a personal training service, you could offer customized training plans based on each customer's fitness goals and abilities.

4.Create Personalized Sales Pitches.

When pitching your products or services to customers, create a personalized sales pitch that addresses their unique needs and preferences. Use the information you have gathered about each customer to tailor your pitch and explain how your product or service can help them achieve their goals. Personalized sales pitches show that you understand and care about each customer's needs.

5.Use Technology to Personalize the Sales Process.

Technology can be a powerful tool for personalization and customization in sales. For example, you can use customer relationship management (CRM) software to track customer interactions and preferences, allowing you to provide a more personalized experience. You can also use chatbots or AI-powered assistants to provide customized recommendations and support to customers.

6.Offer Personalized Discounts and Offers.

Offering personalized discounts and offers is another way to create a personalized experience for your customers. For example, you could offer discounts based on customer purchase history or offer personalized recommendations for related products or services. Personalized discounts and offers show that you value each customer and are willing to provide incentives that meet their unique needs and preferences.

In summary, personalization and customization are essential strategies for creating a personalized and tailored experience for each customer. By gathering information about your customers, using personalized communication, offering customized products and services, creating personalized sales pitches, using technology to personalize the sales process, and offering personalized discounts and offers, you can create a more meaningful and engaging sales process that increases the likelihood of a successful sale.

Additional Tips :

Here are a few additional tips and strategies for personalization and customization in sales:

*Use Segmentation.
Segmentation is the process of dividing your customers into groups based on shared characteristics or behaviors. By segmenting your customers, you can create more targeted and personalized marketing campaigns and sales pitches. For example, you could create segments based on purchase history, interests, or location.

*Offer Personalized Recommendations.
Use customer data and behavior to offer personalized recommendations. For example, if a customer has purchased a specific product, you could recommend related products that they may be interested in. Personalized recommendations can help increase the chances of a successful sale and improve customer satisfaction.

*Provide Personalized Support .
Offer personalized support to your customers throughout the sales process. This can include offering support via phone, email, or chat, and tailoring your support to each customer's specific needs and preferences. Personalized support can help build trust and loyalty with your customers.

*Monitor and Analyze Customer Data.
Continuously monitor and analyze customer data to identify trends and patterns in customer behavior. Use this information to optimize your sales process and improve the customer experience. For example, if you notice that a large number of customers are abandoning their shopping carts, you could investigate the cause and make changes to your sales process to reduce cart abandonment.

*Focus on the Customer Experience.
Ultimately, personalization and customization are about creating a positive and memorable customer experience. Focus on creating a seamless and personalized experience for each customer, from the initial contact through the post-purchase follow-up. By focusing on the customer experience, you can build stronger relationships with your customers and increase the likelihood of repeat business.

In summary, personalization and customization are essential strategies for creating a more personalized and engaging sales process. By using segmentation, offering personalized recommendations and support, monitoring and analyzing customer data, and focusing on the customer experience, you can create a more personalized and effective sales process that drives sales and improves customer satisfaction.

CHAPTER :- 7

Creating a sense of urgency in sales :

Creating a sense of urgency in sales is a strategy that can help increase the chances of a successful sale by encouraging customers to take action quickly. When done effectively, creating a sense of urgency can create a feeling of excitement and urgency in the customer, making them more likely to make a purchase. In this chapter, we'll explore some key strategies for creating a sense of urgency in sales.

1.Limited Time Offers:

Limited time offers are a common strategy for creating a sense of urgency in sales. These offers typically have a set timeframe, such as a weekend sale or a flash sale, and encourage customers to act quickly to take advantage of the offer. By creating a sense of scarcity, limited time offers can increase the perceived value of the product or service and motivate customers to make a purchase.

2.Scarcity :

Scarcity is a powerful psychological principle that can be used to create a sense of urgency in sales. By creating a perception of scarcity, such as limited stock or a limited number of available slots for a service, customers may feel a sense of urgency to act quickly before the product or service is no longer available. Scarcity can create a sense of excitement and competition, making customers more likely to make a purchase.

3.Urgent Messaging :

Urgent messaging is another way to create a sense of urgency in sales. Using messaging that emphasizes the importance of acting quickly, such as "limited time only" or "while supplies last," can create a sense of urgency and encourage customers to take action. Urgent messaging can be used in advertising, email marketing, or on product pages to create a sense of urgency and motivate customers to make a purchase.

4.Exclusivity :

Exclusivity is another way to create a sense of urgency in sales. By offering products or services that are only available to a select group of customers, such as a loyalty program or early access to a new product launch, customers may feel a sense of urgency to take advantage of the exclusive offer before it becomes available to the general public. Exclusivity can create a sense of importance and value, making customers more likely to make a purchase.

5. Social Proof :

Social proof is the idea that people are more likely to take action when they see others doing the same thing. By using social proof, such as customer reviews, ratings, or testimonials, you can create a sense of urgency and motivate customers to make a purchase. When customers see others who have purchased the product or service and are happy with it, they may feel a sense of urgency to make a purchase before the product or service is no longer available.

6.Incentives :

Incentives are another way to create a sense of urgency in sales. By offering incentives such as discounts, free gifts, or exclusive offers, customers may feel a sense of urgency to take advantage of the offer before it expires. Incentives can create a sense of excitement and value, making customers more likely to make a purchase.

In summary, creating a sense of urgency in sales can be an effective strategy for increasing the chances of a successful sale. By using limited time offers, scarcity, urgent messaging, exclusivity, social proof, and incentives, you can create a sense of urgency and motivate customers to take action quickly. However, it is important to use these strategies ethically and responsibly, ensuring that customers feel respected and valued throughout the sales process.

Additional Tips :

Here are a few additional tips and strategies for creating a sense of urgency in sales:

*Use Urgent Language.
Using urgent language in your sales pitch, such as "act now" or "limited quantities available," can create a sense of urgency in the customer. Be careful not to overdo it and come across as too pushy or aggressive, but incorporating urgent language can be effective in creating a sense of excitement and urgency.

*Highlight the Consequences of Delaying.

Another way to create a sense of urgency is to highlight the potential consequences of delaying or not taking action. For example, if you're selling a product that can help solve a problem for the customer, you could highlight the negative impact of not addressing the problem. By emphasizing the consequences of delay, you can motivate customers to take action quickly.

*Use Visuals.
Visuals can be an effective way to create a sense of urgency. For example, using a countdown timer on a product page can create a sense of urgency and motivate customers to make a purchase before the time runs out. Visuals can also be used to highlight scarcity or exclusivity, such as displaying the number of available items left in stock.

*Offer a Bonus.
Offering a bonus or additional incentive for acting quickly can create a sense of urgency and motivate customers to make a purchase. For example, offering a free gift or a discount for customers who purchase within a certain timeframe can create a sense of excitement and urgency.

*Use FOMO (Fear of Missing Out)
FOMO, or fear of missing out, is a powerful psychological principle that can be used to create a sense of urgency. By highlighting the potential benefits of taking action quickly and the negative consequences of delaying, you can create a sense of FOMO and motivate customers to make a purchase before it's too late.

In conclusion, creating a sense of urgency in sales is a powerful strategy that can help increase the chances of a successful sale. By using limited time offers, scarcity, urgent messaging, exclusivity, social proof, incentives, urgent language, highlighting consequences, visuals, offering bonuses, and using FOMO, you can create a sense of excitement and urgency and motivate customers to take action quickly. However, it's important to use these strategies ethically and responsibly and to always prioritize the customer's needs and interests.

CHAPTER :- 8

Leveraging technology for sales success :

Leveraging technology for sales success is becoming increasingly important in today's business world. With technology evolving at a rapid pace, it is essential for sales professionals to stay updated on the latest tools and strategies to succeed. In this chapter, we will discuss the steps that can be taken to leverage technology for sales success.

Step 1: Identify your target audience :

The first step towards leveraging technology for sales success is identifying your target audience. Understanding your audience's needs, preferences, and pain points will help you tailor your sales pitch and ensure that your message resonates with them. Use customer relationship management (CRM) software to keep track of customer information, including contact details, preferences, and previous interactions.

Step 2: Build a strong online presence :

Building a strong online presence is crucial in today's digital age. Your website should be user-friendly, visually appealing, and optimized for search engines. Use social media platforms to connect with your target audience, share valuable content, and build your brand. Utilize email marketing to keep your audience engaged and informed about your products or services.

Step 3: Use data analytics to improve your sales strategy :

Data analytics is a powerful tool that can be used to improve your sales strategy. Analyze customer data to identify patterns, trends, and areas for improvement. Use this information to personalize your sales approach and create targeted marketing campaigns. Additionally, use data analytics to track sales performance, identify areas for improvement, and make data-driven decisions.

Step 4: Utilize automation tools to streamline your sales process :

Automation tools can help streamline your sales process, allowing you to focus on building relationships with your customers. Use automation tools to automate tasks such as lead nurturing, appointment scheduling, and follow-up emails. This will save you time and allow you to focus on high-value tasks, such as building relationships and closing deals.

Step 5: Implement a mobile-friendly strategy:

With mobile usage on the rise, it's essential to implement a mobile-friendly strategy. Your website and marketing materials should be optimized for mobile devices to ensure a seamless user experience. Additionally, use mobile technology to enable remote sales, such as video conferencing and online demos.

Step 6: Invest in AI and machine learning :

AI and machine learning are transforming the sales industry by providing valuable insights into customer behavior and preferences. Utilize AI-powered chatbots to provide 24/7 customer support and automate tasks such as lead qualification. Additionally, use machine learning to analyze sales data and identify patterns and trends.

Step 7: Build a strong network :

Finally, building a strong network is essential for sales success. Attend industry events, participate in online communities, and connect with other professionals in your industry. Use networking tools to keep in touch with your contacts and build relationships with potential customers.

Let's dive a little deeper into each step:

Step 1: Identify your target audience :

Identifying your target audience is the foundation of a successful sales strategy. Use CRM software to collect and manage customer data, including contact information, preferences, and previous interactions. Use this data to segment your audience based on demographics, behavior, and interests. This will help you tailor your sales pitch and create personalized marketing campaigns that resonate with your target audience.

Step 2: Build a strong online presence :

Your website and social media platforms are essential tools for building a strong online presence. Your website should be visually appealing, user-friendly, and optimized for search engines. Use social media platforms such as LinkedIn, Twitter, and Facebook to connect with your target audience, share valuable content, and build your brand.

Email marketing is another effective tool for building an online presence. Use email marketing to keep your audience engaged and informed about your products or services. Create targeted campaigns based on your audience's preferences, behavior, and interests.

Step 3: Use data analytics to improve your sales strategy :

Data analytics provides valuable insights into customer behavior, preferences, and pain points. Use data analytics to analyze customer data and identify patterns, trends, and areas for improvement. Use this information to create targeted marketing campaigns, personalize your sales approach, and make data-driven decisions.

Sales performance analytics can help you track your sales performance, identify areas for improvement, and make data-driven decisions. Use analytics tools to track key performance indicators (KPIs) such as conversion rates, revenue, and customer acquisition costs.

Step 4: Utilize automation tools to streamline your sales process :

Automation tools can help streamline your sales process and improve efficiency. Use automation tools to automate tasks such as lead nurturing, appointment scheduling, and follow-up emails. This will save you time and allow you to focus on high-value tasks, such as building relationships and closing deals.

Chatbots are another effective tool for automating customer support. Use AI-powered chatbots to provide 24/7 customer support and automate tasks such as lead qualification.

Step 5: Implement a mobile-friendly strategy:

With mobile usage on the rise, it's essential to implement a mobile-friendly strategy. Your website and marketing materials should be optimized for mobile devices to ensure a seamless user experience. Additionally, use mobile technology to enable remote sales, such as video conferencing and online demos.

Step 6: Invest in AI and machine learning :

AI and machine learning are transforming the sales industry by providing valuable insights into customer behavior and preferences. Use machine learning to analyze sales data and identify patterns and trends. Use AI-powered chatbots to provide 24/7 customer support and automate tasks such as lead qualification.

Step 7: Build a strong network :

Building a strong network is essential for sales success. Attend industry events, participate in online communities, and connect with other professionals in your industry. Use networking tools to keep in touch with your contacts and build relationships with potential customers.

In conclusion, leveraging technology for sales success requires a strategic approach that incorporates various tools and techniques. By identifying your target audience, building a strong online presence, using data analytics, streamlining your sales process with automation tools, implementing a mobile-friendly strategy, investing in AI and machine learning, and building a strong network, you can position yourself for success in today's competitive business landscape.

Additional Tips:

Here are some additional tips for leveraging technology for sales success:

*.Use social proof:

Social proof is a powerful tool for building trust with potential customers. Use social proof such as customer reviews, case studies, and testimonials to show potential customers that your products or services are effective and reliable.

Personalize your sales approach:
Personalization is key to successful sales. Use customer data to personalize your sales pitch, marketing campaigns, and follow-up emails. This will help you build stronger relationships with potential customers and increase your chances of closing a sale.

Use video marketing: Video marketing is a highly effective tool for engaging potential customers and showcasing your products or services. Use video marketing to create product demos, customer testimonials, and educational content.

Offer value-added services:
Offering value-added services such as free trials, consultations, and demos can help you build trust with potential customers and increase your chances of closing a sale. This also shows that you are committed to providing exceptional customer service.

Use predictive analytics: Predictive analytics can help you identify potential leads and prioritize your sales efforts. Use predictive analytics to analyze customer data and identify potential buyers based on their behavior, interests, and preferences.

Embrace social selling: Social selling involves using social media platforms to connect with potential customers and build relationships. Use social selling to share valuable content, connect with potential customers, and showcase your expertise.

*Use virtual reality (VR) and augmented reality (AR):
VR and AR can help you create immersive product experiences that showcase your products or services in a compelling way. Use VR and AR to create virtual product demos or showcase your products in a 3D environment.

By incorporating these tips into your sales strategy, you can leverage technology to build stronger relationships with potential customers, increase your chances of closing a sale, and position yourself for success in today's competitive business landscape.

CHAPTER :- 9

Tracking and analyzing sales performance data :

Tracking and analyzing sales performance data is essential for identifying areas for improvement and making data-driven decisions. Here are the steps to effectively track and analyze sales performance data:

Step 1: Identify your key performance indicators (KPIs):

Identifying your KPIs is the first step to effectively tracking and analyzing sales performance data. KPIs are metrics that measure your performance and help you identify areas for improvement. Some common KPIs for sales include conversion rates, revenue, customer acquisition costs, and customer retention rates.

Step 2: Collect sales data :

Once you've identified your KPIs, you need to collect sales data. This includes data on sales volume, revenue, customer demographics, and product performance. Use a CRM system to collect and manage this data. This will allow you to easily track your performance and identify areas for improvement.

Step 3: Analyze your sales data :

Once you've collected your sales data, you need to analyze it. Use data visualization tools such as charts and graphs to analyze your data and identify trends and patterns. Look for areas where you are performing well, as well as areas where you need to improve.

Step 4: Identify areas for improvement :

Use your sales data to identify areas for improvement. Look for trends or patterns that indicate potential problems or opportunities. For example, if you have a low conversion rate, you may need to improve your sales pitch or offer better incentives to potential customers.

Step 5: Develop an action plan :

Once you've identified areas for improvement, you need to develop an action plan. This plan should include specific goals and strategies for improving your performance. For example, if you need to improve your conversion rate, you may develop a plan to improve your sales pitch or offer better incentives to potential customers.

Step 6: Implement your action plan :

Once you've developed your action plan, you need to implement it. This may involve training your sales team, improving your marketing campaigns, or changing your sales approach. Be sure to track your progress and adjust your plan as needed.

Step 7: Monitor and evaluate your results :

Finally, you need to monitor and evaluate your results. Use your CRM system to track your progress and measure your success. Look for trends or patterns that indicate whether your actions are having the desired effect. If you're not seeing the results you want, you may need to adjust your action plan or try a different approach.

More in-depth discussions of the above steps.

Tracking and analyzing sales performance data is a crucial part of any successful sales strategy. Here's a more in-depth look at each of the steps involved:

Step 1: Identify your key performance indicators (KPIs)

Identifying your KPIs is the first step in tracking and analyzing sales performance data. KPIs are metrics that help you measure the success of your sales efforts. Common KPIs for sales include conversion rates, revenue, customer acquisition costs, and customer retention rates.

To identify your KPIs, start by considering your business objectives. What are you trying to achieve with your sales efforts? Once you've identified your objectives, consider the metrics that will help you measure your progress towards those objectives.

Step 2: Collect sales data.

Once you've identified your KPIs, you need to collect sales data. This includes data on sales volume, revenue, customer demographics, and product performance. The best way to collect this data is by using a CRM system. A CRM system allows you to centralize your sales data, making it easier to manage and analyze.

When collecting sales data, make sure you're collecting data from all relevant sources. This may include your website analytics, sales reports, and customer feedback.

Step 3: Analyze your sales data.

Once you've collected your sales data, you need to analyze it. Data visualization tools such as charts and graphs can help you analyze your data and identify trends and patterns. Look for areas where you're performing well, as well as areas where you need to improve.

When analyzing your sales data, consider the context. For example, if you notice a spike in sales for a particular product, consider whether this was due to a marketing campaign or a change in customer behavior.

Step 4: Identify areas for improvement.

Once you've analyzed your sales data, you should have a good understanding of your performance. Use this information to identify areas for improvement. Look for trends or patterns that indicate potential problems or opportunities.

When identifying areas for improvement, consider the impact each area will have on your overall sales performance. Prioritize areas that will have the biggest impact.

Step 5: Develop an action plan.

Once you've identified areas for improvement, you need to develop an action plan. This plan should include specific goals and strategies for improving your performance. For example, if you need to improve your conversion rate, you may develop a plan to improve your sales pitch or offer better incentives to potential customers.

When developing your action plan, make sure you're setting SMART goals. SMART goals are Specific, Measurable, Achievable, Relevant, and Time-bound.

Step 6: Implement your action plan.

Once you've developed your action plan, you need to implement it. This may involve training your sales team, improving your marketing campaigns, or changing your sales approach. Be sure to track your progress and adjust your plan as needed.

When implementing your action plan, make sure you're communicating the plan to all relevant stakeholders. This may include your sales team, marketing team, and customer service team.

Step 7: Monitor and evaluate your results.

Finally, you need to monitor and evaluate your results. Use your CRM system to track your progress and measure your success. Look for trends or patterns that indicate whether your actions are having the desired effect. If you're not seeing the results you want, you may need to adjust your action plan or try a different approach.

When evaluating your results, make sure you're using the right metrics. For example, if you're trying to improve your customer retention rate, you may need to look at metrics such as customer satisfaction and customer loyalty.

By following these steps, you can effectively track and analyze your sales performance data and make data-driven decisions that improve your performance and increase your revenue. Remember to regularly review and adjust your strategies based on your performance data to ensure that you continue to improve and stay ahead of the competition.

Additional Tips :

Here are some additional tips for tracking and analyzing sales performance data:

*Use segmentation:** Segmenting your sales data allows you to analyze specific groups of customers or products. This can help you identify trends and patterns that are not apparent when looking at your overall sales data. For example, you may segment your data by customer demographics or product categories.

*Benchmark your performance: Benchmarking your performance against industry standards or competitors can help you identify areas where you are falling behind or excelling. This can help you set realistic goals and develop effective strategies for improvement.

*Use predictive analytics: Predictive analytics can help you identify patterns in your sales data that may not be immediately apparent. Use predictive analytics to forecast future sales, identify potential customer churn, and optimize your pricing strategies.

*Analyze customer behavior:
Analyzing customer behavior can help you identify areas where you can improve your sales and marketing efforts. Look at factors such as the time of day customers are most likely to make a purchase, the types of products customers are most interested in, and the channels they prefer to use.

*Use A/B testing:
A/B testing involves testing two versions of a sales pitch, marketing campaign, or product feature to see which performs better. Use A/B testing to optimize your sales and marketing efforts and improve your conversion rates.

*Track your pipeline: Tracking your pipeline involves monitoring your sales opportunities and their progress through the sales funnel. Use a CRM system to track your pipeline and identify areas where you may need to focus your efforts.

By incorporating these tips into your sales performance data tracking and analysis strategy, you can gain deeper insights into your sales performance, identify areas for improvement, and make data-driven decisions that lead to increased revenue and growth.

CHAPTER :- 10

Developing a strong brand image and reputation :

Developing a strong brand image and reputation is crucial for the success of any business. A positive reputation can attract new customers, retain existing ones, and increase brand loyalty. In this chapter, we will discuss step-by-step how to develop a strong brand image and reputation.

Step 1: Define your brand's values and mission :
The first step in developing a strong brand image and reputation is to define your brand's values and mission. Your brand's values are the beliefs and principles that guide your business, while your mission statement is a concise statement that outlines your business's purpose and objectives. It's important to clearly define these aspects of your brand as they will guide all future actions and decisions.

Step 2: Identify your target audience :
The second step in developing a strong brand image and reputation is to identify your target audience. Your target audience is the group of people who are most likely to be interested in your product or service. Understanding your target audience's needs, wants, and preferences will help you create a brand that resonates with them.

Step 3: Create a strong brand identity :
Your brand identity is the visual and tangible representation of your brand. It includes your brand name, logo, tagline, and any other visual elements that make your brand easily identifiable. Creating a strong brand identity that accurately reflects your brand's values and mission is crucial in developing a strong brand image and reputation.

Step 4: Develop a consistent brand voice :
Your brand voice is the tone and style in which you communicate with your target audience. It includes the language you use in your advertising, marketing, and social media. Developing a consistent brand voice that resonates with your target audience is key in building a strong brand image and reputation.

Step 5: Provide excellent customer service :
Providing excellent customer service is one of the most important aspects of building a strong brand image and reputation. Consistently delivering high-quality products or services and treating your customers with respect and

empathy will go a long way in creating a positive reputation for your brand.

Step 6: Build strong relationships with your customers :

Building strong relationships with your customers is another important factor in developing a strong brand image and reputation. Engage with your customers on social media, respond to their inquiries promptly, and listen to their feedback. By showing your customers that you value their input, you can build a loyal customer base that will help spread positive word-of-mouth about your brand.

Step 7: Leverage social media :

Social media is a powerful tool for building a strong brand image and reputation. Use social media to engage with your target audience, promote your brand's values and mission, and showcase your products or services. By consistently posting high-quality content that resonates with your target audience, you can build a strong following and increase brand loyalty.

Step 8: Partner with other reputable brands :

Partnering with other reputable brands can help enhance your brand's reputation. Collaborating with brands that share your values and mission can help you reach new audiences and build credibility within your industry.

Step 9: Deliver on your promises :

Delivering on your promises is crucial in building a strong brand image and reputation. Be honest and transparent in your marketing and advertising, and consistently deliver high-quality products or services. By consistently meeting or exceeding your customers' expectations, you can build a positive reputation for your brand.

Step 10: Monitor and manage your brand reputation : Finally, it's important to monitor and manage your brand reputation. Regularly check customer reviews and social media mentions to ensure that your brand is being perceived positively. If you receive negative feedback, respond promptly and take steps to address the issue. By actively managing your brand reputation, you can ensure that your brand is perceived positively by your target audience.

In conclusion, developing a strong brand image and reputation is essential for the success of any business. By defining your brand's values and mission, identifying your target audience, creating a strong brand identity and voice, providing excellent customer service, building strong relationships with your customers, leveraging social media, partnering with other reputable brands, delivering on your promises, and monitoring and managing your brand reputation, you can build a positive and enduring brand image and reputation.

It's important to note that building a strong brand image and reputation is a continuous process that requires ongoing effort and attention. By consistently living up to your brand's values and mission, listening to and engaging with your customers, and adapting to changes in the market, you can ensure that your brand remains relevant and resonates with your target audience.

In today's highly competitive business landscape, developing a strong brand image and reputation is more important than ever. By following the steps outlined in this article, you can build a brand that not only stands out from the competition but also attracts and retains loyal customers who will advocate for your brand and help drive its success.

Additional Tips :

Specifically, some additional tips and strategies for developing a strong brand image and reputation are as follows :

*Offer unique and valuable products or services.
One of the best ways to build a strong brand image and reputation is to offer unique and valuable products or services that are difficult to find elsewhere. By offering something that stands out from the competition, you can attract new customers and build a loyal customer base that will help spread positive word-of-mouth about your brand.

*Be socially responsible.
Consumers today are increasingly interested in supporting brands that are socially responsible and environmentally conscious. By demonstrating a commitment to social and environmental issues that are important to your target

audience, you can build a positive reputation for your brand and attract customers who share your values.

*Establish thought leadership.
Establishing thought leadership within your industry can help enhance your brand's reputation and credibility. By sharing your expertise and insights through blog posts, white papers, webinars, and other content, you can position your brand as a trusted authority in your industry and build a loyal following of customers and fans.

*Participate in industry events and conferences.
Participating in industry events and conferences can help increase your brand's visibility and credibility within your industry. By attending and speaking at events, you can network with other industry professionals, share your expertise and insights, and promote your brand to a wider audience.

*Invest in employee training and development.
Your employees are the face of your brand, and investing in their training and development can help ensure that they represent your brand in a positive and professional manner. By providing ongoing training and development opportunities, you can help your employees deliver exceptional customer service and build strong relationships with your customers.

In summary, developing a strong brand image and reputation requires a multifaceted approach that involves defining your brand's values and mission, identifying your target audience, creating a strong brand identity and voice, providing excellent customer service, building strong relationships with your customers, leveraging social media, partnering with other reputable brands, delivering on your promises, monitoring and managing your brand reputation, and implementing additional strategies such as offering unique and valuable products or services, being socially responsible, establishing thought leadership, participating in industry events and conferences, and investing in employee training and development. By following these strategies and continuously adapting to changes in the market, you can build a brand that is not only successful but also respected and admired by your target audience.

CHAPTER :- 11

Staying up-to-date with the latest sales trends and techniques:

Staying up-to-date with the latest sales trends and techniques is essential for any business looking to remain competitive and successful in today's fast-paced and ever-changing marketplace. In this chapter, we will provide you with step-by-step instructions on how to stay informed about the latest sales trends and techniques.

Step 1: Attend Industry Conferences and Trade Shows :

One of the best ways to stay up-to-date with the latest sales trends and techniques is to attend industry conferences and trade shows. These events bring together sales professionals, thought leaders, and industry experts to discuss the latest trends and best practices in the field. By attending these events, you can network with other professionals, learn about new products and services, and gain valuable insights into the latest sales techniques.

Step 2: Read Industry Publications and Blogs :

Another great way to stay informed about the latest sales trends and techniques is to read industry publications and blogs. There are many trade publications and blogs that are dedicated to sales and marketing, and they often provide in-depth analysis and insights into the latest trends and best practices in the field. By subscribing to these publications and blogs, you can stay up-to-date on the latest developments and learn from other professionals in the industry.

Step 3: Join Professional Associations :

Joining a professional association is another effective way to stay informed about the latest sales trends and techniques. These organizations bring together sales professionals from different industries and provide a forum for networking, education, and professional development. By joining a professional association, you can attend industry events, participate in training programs, and connect with other sales professionals who share your interests and goals.

Step 4: Participate in Online Sales Communities :

In addition to attending industry events and joining professional associations, participating in online sales communities is another effective way to stay informed about the latest sales trends and techniques. There are many online forums, social media groups, and LinkedIn communities that are dedicated to sales and marketing. By participating in these communities, you can connect with other sales professionals, share ideas and best practices, and stay informed about the latest developments in the field.

Step 5: Attend Training and Development Programs :

Attending training and development programs is another important step in staying up-to-date with the latest sales trends and techniques. There are many training programs available that focus on different aspects of sales and marketing, including lead generation, customer acquisition, and closing deals. By attending these programs, you can learn new skills and techniques, network with other professionals, and gain valuable insights into the latest sales trends and best practices.

Step 6: Analyze Sales Data :

Analyzing sales data is an important step in staying up-to-date with the latest sales trends and techniques. By analyzing your sales data, you can identify patterns and trends in your sales performance and gain insights into what is working and what is not. You can use this information to make data-driven decisions and adjust your sales strategy accordingly.

Step 7: Conduct Market Research :

Conducting market research is another effective way to stay informed about the latest sales trends and techniques. By conducting market research, you can gather information about your target audience, competitors, and industry trends. You can use this information to develop a deeper understanding of your market and identify opportunities for growth and improvement.

Step 8: Seek Out Mentors and Advisors :

Seeking out mentors and advisors is another valuable way to stay up-to-date with the latest sales trends and techniques. Mentors and advisors can provide guidance, support, and advice based on their experience and expertise. They can help you navigate challenges and identify opportunities for growth and improvement.

Step 9: Experiment with New Techniques :

Experimenting with new techniques is another effective way to stay up-to-date with the latest sales trends and techniques. By trying out new techniques, you can test their effectiveness and determine whether they are a good fit for your business. You can also learn from your successes and failures and use this knowledge to refine your sales strategy.

Step 10: Embrace Technology :

Finally, embracing technology is an important step in staying up-to-date with the latest sales trends and techniques. Technology is constantly evolving, and there are many tools and platforms available that can help you streamline your sales process, improve your efficiency, and enhance your customer experience. By embracing technology, you can stay ahead of the curve and position your business for success.

In conclusion, staying up-to-date with the latest sales trends and techniques is essential for any business looking to remain competitive and successful in today's marketplace. By attending industry conferences and trade shows, reading industry publications and blogs, joining professional associations, participating in online sales communities, and attending training and development programs, you can stay informed about the latest developments and gain valuable insights into the latest sales techniques. By incorporating these strategies into your sales strategy, you can improve your sales performance, grow your business, and achieve greater success in the marketplace.

Additional Tips :

Here are some additional tips for staying up-to-date with the latest sales trends and techniques:

*Attend webinars and online training courses:
In addition to attending industry conferences and trade shows, webinars and online training courses are a great way to learn about the latest sales trends and techniques from the comfort of your own home or office. Many industry experts and thought leaders offer online training and webinars on topics such as sales techniques, lead generation, and customer engagement.

*Network with other sales professionals:
Networking with other sales professionals is a great way to stay informed about the latest sales trends and techniques. You can join networking groups on LinkedIn or attend local meetups to connect with other sales professionals in your area. You can exchange ideas, share best practices, and learn from one another's experiences.

*Read books and articles: There are many books and articles written by sales experts and thought leaders that can provide valuable insights into the latest sales trends and techniques. You can read books on topics such as sales psychology, sales techniques, and sales leadership to learn about the latest developments in the field.

*Follow industry influencers on social media:

Many industry influencers share their insights and opinions on social media platforms such as Twitter and LinkedIn. You can follow these influencers to stay informed about the latest developments in the field and learn from their experiences and expertise.

*Conduct A/B testing:
A/B testing is a valuable technique that can help you identify the most effective sales techniques for your business. By testing different sales strategies on a small scale, you can determine which techniques are most effective and refine your sales strategy accordingly.

*Solicit feedback from customers:
Soliciting feedback from your customers is a great way to stay informed about their preferences and needs. By listening to their feedback, you can identify opportunities for improvement and adjust your sales strategy to better meet their needs.

*Attend sales training workshops:
Sales training workshops are designed to help sales professionals develop new skills and techniques. Attending these workshops can provide you with valuable insights into the latest sales trends and techniques and help you improve your sales performance.

*Keep track of your competitors:
Keeping track of your competitors can help you stay informed about the latest sales trends and techniques in your industry. You can monitor their sales strategies, marketing campaigns, and customer engagement techniques to learn from their successes and failures.

In conclusion, staying up-to-date with the latest sales trends and techniques requires a commitment to learning, experimentation, and adaptation.

By following these additional tips, you can stay informed about the latest developments in the field and position your business for success in the marketplace.

CHAPTER :- 12

The importance of active listening in sales :

Active listening is a critical skill for sales professionals to master. Active listening involves paying close attention to what the customer is saying, both verbally and non-verbally, and using that information to build rapport, establish trust, and ultimately close the sale. In this chapter, we will outline the importance of active listening in sales and provide a step-by-step guide to mastering this important skill.

Step 1: Understand the Importance of Active Listening :

Active listening is important in sales for several reasons.

First, it allows you to build rapport with the customer by demonstrating that you are truly interested in their needs and concerns.

Second, it helps you establish trust with the customer by showing that you are listening to their feedback and taking it into account when making recommendations.

Finally, active listening enables you to identify the customer's pain points and tailor your sales pitch to address those specific needs.

Step 2: Eliminate Distractions :

To engage in active listening, it is important to eliminate distractions and focus solely on the customer. This means turning off your phone, closing your laptop, and eliminating any other distractions that may interfere with your ability to listen attentively.

Step 3: Use Non-Verbal Cues :

Non-verbal cues, such as nodding your head, maintaining eye contact, and using appropriate facial expressions, are important components of active listening. These cues demonstrate to the customer that you are fully engaged in the conversation and are focused on their needs.

Step 4: Ask Open-Ended Questions :

Asking open-ended questions is a key component of active listening. Open-ended questions encourage the customer to share their thoughts and feelings, and allow you to gather more detailed information about their needs and concerns. Examples of open-ended questions include "What are your goals for this product/service?" and "Can you tell me more about your experience with our competitors?"

Step 5: Paraphrase and Summarize :

Paraphrasing and summarizing what the customer has said is another important component of active listening. This demonstrates that you have been listening attentively and have a clear understanding of the customer's needs and concerns. It also allows you to clarify any misunderstandings and ensure that you are both on the same page.

Step 6: Use Active Listening to Address Objections :

Active listening can also be a valuable tool for addressing objections. When a customer raises an objection, actively listening to their concerns and responding with empathy can help you overcome their objections and close the sale. By demonstrating that you understand their concerns and are committed to finding a solution that meets their needs, you can build trust and establish a stronger relationship with the customer.

Step 7: Practice Active Listening :

Like any skill, active listening requires practice to master. You can practice active listening by engaging in role-playing exercises with colleagues, listening to podcasts or webinars on the topic, or simply practicing active listening in your everyday interactions with others.

In conclusion, active listening is a critical skill for sales professionals to master. By eliminating distractions, using non-verbal cues, asking open-ended questions, paraphrasing and summarizing, and using active listening to address objections, you can build rapport, establish trust, and ultimately close more sales. By practicing active listening in your daily interactions, you can become a more effective sales professional and achieve greater success in your career.

Additional Tips :

Here are some additional tips for mastering active listening in sales:

*Use the Customer's Name.
Using the customer's name during the conversation can help establish a personal connection and make them feel valued. Addressing them by their name can also help you remember their name for future interactions, which can help strengthen the relationship.

*Avoid Interrupting.
Interrupting the customer can make them feel disrespected and may cause them to lose interest in the conversation. Allow

them to finish speaking before responding, and avoid jumping to conclusions or making assumptions.

*Be Present .
Being fully present in the conversation means focusing on the customer and their needs, rather than thinking about your next response or getting distracted by other things. This requires concentration and mental effort, but can ultimately lead to a more successful sales outcome.

*Use Mirroring.
Mirroring involves repeating back what the customer has said using their own words. This technique shows the customer that you are truly listening to their concerns and can help you better understand their needs.

*Practice Empathy.
Empathy involves understanding and acknowledging the customer's feelings and concerns. By practicing empathy, you can build a stronger rapport with the customer and establish trust, which can ultimately lead to more successful sales outcomes.

*Follow Up.
After the conversation, follow up with the customer to ensure that their needs were met and that they are satisfied with the outcome. This can help reinforce the relationship and increase the likelihood of future sales.

In conclusion, mastering active listening is essential for sales professionals who want to build strong relationships with customers and close more sales. By using the customer's name, avoiding interruptions, being present, using mirroring, practicing empathy, and following up, you can become a more effective listener and ultimately achieve greater success in your career.

CHAPTER :- 13

Using data and analytics to make informed sales decisions :

In today's business world, making informed sales decisions is critical to the success of any organization. One of the best ways to achieve this is by using data and analytics to inform your decision-making process. In this chapter, we'll explore the steps involved in using data and analytics to make informed sales decisions.

Step 1: Define Your Goals :

The first step in using data and analytics to make informed sales decisions is to define your goals. This means identifying the key performance indicators (KPIs) that are most important to your business. These might include metrics like revenue, profit margin, customer retention rate, or conversion rate. Once you've identified your KPIs, you can begin collecting and analyzing data to track your progress towards these goals.

Step 2: Collect Data :

The next step is to collect the data you need to inform your sales decisions. This might involve gathering data from a variety of sources, including sales reports, customer feedback surveys, website analytics, and social media metrics. It's important to ensure that the data you collect is accurate, relevant, and up-to-date.

Step 3: Analyze Data :

Once you have collected your data, the next step is to analyze it. This involves using data analytics tools and techniques to identify patterns, trends, and insights that can help you make informed sales decisions. For example, you might use data visualization tools to create charts and graphs that illustrate your sales performance over time, or use predictive analytics to forecast future sales trends.

Step 4: Identify Opportunities :

Once you have analyzed your data, you can begin identifying opportunities for improvement. This might involve identifying areas where you are underperforming, or spotting trends that suggest new sales opportunities. For example, you might notice that sales are consistently low during a particular time of day, which could suggest that you need to adjust your marketing strategy to better target that time period.

Step 5: Develop Action Plans :

Once you have identified opportunities for improvement, the next step is to develop action plans to capitalize on these opportunities. This might involve making changes to your sales processes, adjusting your marketing strategy, or introducing new products or services to your customers. It's important to develop clear, specific action plans that are designed to achieve your sales goals.

Step 6: Implement Changes :

Once you have developed your action plans, the next step is to implement the changes you have identified. This might involve training your sales team on new processes or introducing new products to your customers. It's important to track your progress as you implement these changes to ensure that they are having the desired impact on your sales performance.

Step 7: Monitor Results :

Finally, it's important to monitor your results as you implement your changes. This means continuing to collect and analyze data to track your progress towards your sales goals. It also means adjusting your action plans as needed to ensure that you are achieving the desired results.

In conclusion, using data and analytics to make informed sales decisions is a powerful tool for any business looking to improve their sales performance. By defining your goals, collecting and analyzing data, identifying opportunities, developing action plans, implementing changes, and monitoring your results, you can make informed decisions that drive your business forward. So, if you want to stay ahead of the competition and achieve your sales goals, start leveraging the power of data and analytics today!

Additional Tips :

Here are some additional tips to help you use data and analytics to make informed sales decisions:

*Use a variety of data sources -
Don't rely on just one source of data. By using multiple sources of data, you can get a more complete picture of your sales performance and identify opportunities for improvement that might otherwise go unnoticed.

*Use data visualization tools -
Data visualization tools, such as charts and graphs, can help you easily identify trends and patterns in your data. This can make it easier to identify areas where you need to focus your attention.

*Use predictive analytics - Predictive analytics can help you forecast future sales trends and identify potential opportunities for growth. By using historical data to develop predictive models, you can make more accurate predictions about future sales performance.

*Get buy-in from your sales team -
Using data and analytics to inform your sales decisions can be a big change for your sales team. It's important to get their buy-in and support, and to involve them in the process of developing and implementing action plans.

*Continuously monitor and adjust -
Sales performance is not static, and neither is the data that informs your decisions. It's important to continuously monitor your results and adjust your strategies as needed to ensure that you're achieving your goals.

By following these tips, you can make the most of data and analytics to inform your sales decisions and achieve your sales goals.

CHAPTER :- 14

Staying motivated and focused in sales :

Selling can be a challenging and often unpredictable profession, which can make it difficult to stay motivated and focused. However, there are several strategies you can use to maintain your motivation and focus and achieve your sales goals. In this chapter, we'll discuss, how to stay motivated and focused in sales, step by steps :

1.Set clear and achievable goals -
Having clear goals can give you direction and motivation. Make sure your goals are specific, measurable, and achievable, and break them down into smaller milestones to make them more manageable.

2.Develop a positive mindset -
A positive mindset can help you stay motivated even when things get tough. Focus on your strengths, celebrate your successes, and learn from your failures.

3.Stay organized - Staying organized can help you stay on top of your sales activities and priorities. Use a calendar or task list to keep track of your appointments, follow-ups, and deadlines.

4.Focus on building relationships -
Building relationships with your customers can help you maintain motivation and focus, as well as improve your sales performance. Take the time to get to know your customers, listen to their needs, and provide personalized solutions.

5.Embrace rejection - Rejection is a natural part of sales, and it's important to learn how to handle it. Don't take rejection personally, and use it as an opportunity to learn and improve your sales approach.

6.Continuously learn and improve -

Sales is a constantly evolving profession, and it's important to stay up to date with the latest trends and techniques. Attend training sessions, read industry publications, and seek feedback from your colleagues and customers.

7.Take breaks and manage stress -

Taking breaks and managing stress can help you avoid burnout and maintain focus. Take regular breaks throughout the day, and engage in activities that help you relax, such as exercise or meditation.

8.Stay accountable - Staying accountable can help you stay motivated and focused. Set up regular check-ins with a colleague or mentor, and use these sessions to review your progress, set new goals, and discuss any challenges or roadblocks.

By following these steps, you can stay motivated and focused in sales and achieve your sales goals. Remember, selling is a dynamic and challenging profession, but with the right mindset and approach, you can succeed and thrive in your sales career.

Additional Tips :

Here are some additional tips to help you stay motivated and focused in sales:

*Use positive affirmations - Positive affirmations can help you develop a positive mindset and boost your confidence. Repeat positive affirmations to yourself throughout the day, such as "I am a successful salesperson" or "I can handle any challenge that comes my way."

*Celebrate small successes -
Celebrate every small success, such as closing a sale or making a good impression on a customer. This can help you stay motivated and positive, and build momentum towards achieving your larger goals.

*Stay connected with colleagues -
Staying connected with your colleagues can help you stay motivated and focused, and provide you with valuable support and advice. Attend team meetings, participate in team-building activities, and reach out to colleagues for help when you need it.

*Use visualization techniques -
Visualization techniques can help you visualize your success and stay motivated. Visualize yourself achieving your goals, making successful sales, and overcoming challenges.

*Focus on the customer - Focusing on the customer can help you stay motivated and focused, and improve your sales performance. Put yourself in the customer's shoes, and think about how you can provide them with the best possible solution to their needs.

*Stay up to date with technology -
Staying up to date with the latest sales technology can help you work more efficiently, and stay competitive in the marketplace. Attend training sessions, read industry

publications, and learn about new tools and techniques that can help you improve your sales performance.

*Take care of yourself - Taking care of yourself is essential to staying motivated and focused in sales. Make sure you're getting enough sleep, eating a healthy diet, and taking breaks throughout the day to recharge your batteries.

By following these additional tips, you can stay motivated and focused in sales and achieve your sales goals. Remember, maintaining a positive mindset, staying organized, and focusing on the customer can help you overcome challenges and succeed in your sales career.

CHAPTER :- 15

Overcoming common sales challenges and obstacles :

As a salesperson, you're likely to face a range of challenges and obstacles that can make your job difficult. However, with the right approach, you can overcome these obstacles and achieve your sales goals. In this chapter, we'll outline some common sales challenges and provide step-by-step guidance on how to overcome them.

1.Difficulty Generating Leads :

Generating leads can be challenging, but it's an essential part of the sales process. To generate leads effectively, you should:

- **Define your target audience:**
  Understand who your ideal customer is and what their needs and pain points are.

- **Use multiple channels:**
  Use a variety of channels such as social media, email marketing, and networking events to reach potential customers.

- **Provide value:**
  Offer helpful content such as blogs, e-books, and webinars that address your target audience's pain points and offer solutions.

- **Be persistent:**
  Follow up with leads regularly and stay top of mind with potential customers.

2.Rejection :

Salespeople face rejection regularly, which can be discouraging. However, rejection is a natural part of the sales process, and it's important to develop resilience to overcome it.

To overcome rejection, you should:

- **Reframe your mindset:**

Instead of seeing rejection as a failure, see it as an opportunity to learn and improve.

- **Focus on the positive:**
  Celebrate small wins, such as successful cold calls or meetings, to stay motivated.

- **Ask for feedback:**
  Ask prospects who declined your offer for feedback on why they did so. Use this feedback to improve your approach.

- **Keep a positive attitude:**
  Stay positive and enthusiastic, even in the face of rejection.

3.Handling Objections :

Objections are common in sales, but they can be difficult to handle. To handle objections effectively, you should:

- **Listen actively:**
  Allow the prospect to express their concerns fully and actively listen to what they're saying.

- **Acknowledge the objection:**
  Show that you understand and respect their concerns.

- **Address the objection:**
  Provide a response that addresses their concerns and offers a solution.

- **Ask for feedback:**
  Ask the prospect if your response addressed their concerns and if there are any other objections you should be aware of.

4.Closing Sales :

Closing sales is the ultimate goal of the sales process, but it can be difficult to achieve. To close sales effectively, you should:

- **Build rapport:**
  Develop a relationship with the prospect based on trust and mutual understanding.

- **Understand their needs:**
  Identify the prospect's pain points and how your product or service can solve them.

- **Offer value:**
  Highlight the benefits of your product or service and how it can help the prospect.

- **Create urgency:**
  Show the prospect why they need to act now and not delay their decision.

- **Ask for the sale:**
  Finally, ask for the sale and close the deal.

5.Managing Time :

Salespeople often have a lot on their plates, from generating leads to following up with prospects to closing sales. To manage your time effectively, you should:

- **Prioritize:**
  Identify the most important tasks and focus on them first.

- **Set goals:**
  Set specific, measurable goals and develop a plan to achieve them.

- **Automate:** Use technology such as scheduling software and email templates to streamline your workflow.

- **Delegate:**
  Outsource or delegate tasks that are not essential to your core sales responsibilities.

6.Staying Motivated :
Sales can be a challenging and demanding job, which can lead to burnout and demotivation. To stay motivated, you should:

- **Celebrate wins:**
  Take time to acknowledge and celebrate your successes, no matter how small.

- **Set goals:**
  Set challenging but achievable goals to give yourself a sense of purpose and direction.

- **Stay positive:**
  Focus on the positive aspects of your job and maintain a positive attitude.

- **Take breaks:**
  Take breaks throughout the day to refresh and recharge your energy levels. It's important to take breaks so you can come back to your work with a clear and focused mind.

- **Seek support:**
  Connect with colleagues, mentors, or a support group to share ideas, vent frustrations, and gain perspective.

- **Learn new skills:** Continuously develop your sales skills and knowledge through reading, training courses, or mentorship.

7.Adapting to Change :

The sales landscape is constantly evolving, and salespeople need to be adaptable to stay ahead. To adapt to change, you should:

- **Stay informed:**
  Keep up to date with industry news, trends, and changes in your target market.

- **Experiment:**

Try new sales techniques and strategies to see what works best for you and your customers.

- **Be flexible:**
  Be willing to change your approach and pivot when necessary to meet changing customer needs or market conditions.

- **Learn from failures:**
  Don't be afraid to experiment and take risks, but also learn from your failures and adjust your approach accordingly.

In conclusion, sales can be a challenging and rewarding career, but it's important to develop the right mindset and skills to overcome common challenges and obstacles.

By following the steps outlined above, you can generate more leads, handle objections effectively, close more sales, manage your time, stay motivated, and adapt to change. Remember to stay persistent, seek feedback, and continuously develop your skills to achieve long-term success in sales.

Additional Tips :

Here are some additional tips that can help you overcome common sales challenges and obstacles:

1.Build relationships: Sales is all about building relationships with customers, prospects, and colleagues. Take the time to understand their needs, interests, and goals, and develop a rapport based on trust and mutual respect.

2.Use data:
Data can provide valuable insights into your customers, market trends, and sales performance. Use data to identify patterns, spot opportunities, and make informed decisions about your sales strategy.

3.Practice active listening: Active listening is a skill that can help you understand your customers' needs and concerns. Practice active listening by asking open-ended questions, paraphrasing what they say, and clarifying any misunderstandings.

4.Personalize your approach:
Customers want to feel understood and valued. Personalize your approach by tailoring your sales pitch to their specific needs and interests, and using their name in your communication.

5.Follow up:
Following up with prospects and customers is crucial for building relationships and closing sales. Set reminders to follow up at regular intervals, and use personalized communication to stay top of mind.

6.Be persistent: Persistence is key in sales. Don't give up after the first rejection or objection. Follow up consistently and look for ways to address their concerns and provide value.

7.Collaborate:

Sales is a team effort. Collaborate with your colleagues, marketing team, and other departments to share knowledge, resources, and best practices.

8.Learn from your mistakes:
Sales is a learning process. Don't be afraid to make mistakes, but also don't repeat them. Learn from your failures, and use them as opportunities to improve and grow.

9.Stay organized:
Sales can be hectic and fast-paced. Stay organized by using tools like a CRM system, to-do lists, and calendar reminders. Being organized can help you stay focused and manage your time more effectively.

10.Keep up with industry trends:
The sales landscape is constantly evolving. Stay informed about new products, services, and industry trends that may impact your customers and your sales strategy.

By following these additional tips, you can improve your sales performance, overcome common challenges, and achieve your sales goals. Remember, sales is a process that requires patience, persistence, and continuous learning.

www.ingramcontent.com/pod-product-compliance
Lightning Source LLC
Chambersburg PA
CBHW071139220526
45467CB00015B/1510